Learning to Read, Step by Step!

Ready to Read **Preschool–Kindergarten**
• big type and easy words • rhyme and rhythm • picture clues
For children who know the alphabet and are eager to begin reading.

Reading with Help **Preschool–Grade 1**
• basic vocabulary • short sentences • simple stories
For children who recognize familiar words and sound out new words with help.

Reading on Your Own **Grades 1–3**
• engaging characters • easy-to-follow plots • popular topics
For children who are ready to read on their own.

Reading Paragraphs **Grades 2–3**
• challenging vocabulary • short paragraphs • exciting stories
For newly independent readers who read simple sentences with confidence.

Ready for Chapters **Grades 2–4**
• chapters • longer paragraphs • full-color art
For children who want to take the plunge into chapter books but still like colorful pictures.

STEP INTO READING® is designed to give every child a successful reading experience. The grade levels are only guides; children will progress through the steps at their own speed, developing confidence in their reading. The F&P Text Level on the back cover serves as another tool to help you choose the right book for your child.

Remember, a lifetime love of reading starts with a single step!

Visit us on the Web!
StepIntoReading.com
rhcbooks.com

Educators and librarians, for a variety of teaching tools, visit us at RHTeachersLibrarians.com

Library of Congress Cataloging-in-Publication Data
Names: Krensky, Stephen, author. | Green, Norman, illustrator.
Title: Christopher Columbus : explorer and colonist / by Stephen Krensky ; illustrated by Norman Green.
Description: New York : Random House Children's Books, [2020] | Series: Step into reading ; Step 3 | Audience: Grades 2–3 | Audience: Ages 5–8 | Summary: "An early reader biography focusing on Christopher Columbus" —Provided by publisher.
Identifiers: LCCN 2020000093 (print) | LCCN 2020000094 (ebook) | ISBN 978-0-593-18173-7 (trade paperback) | ISBN 978-0-593-18174-4 (library binding) | ISBN 978-0-593-18175-1 (ebook)
Subjects: LCSH: Columbus, Christopher—Juvenile literature. | America—Discovery and exploration—Spanish—Juvenile literature.
Classification: LCC E118 .K74 2020 (print) | LCC E118 (ebook) | DDC 970.01/5092 [B]—dc23

Printed in the United States of America
10 9 8 7 6 5 4 3 2 1

This book has been officially leveled by using the F&P Text Level Gradient™ Leveling System.

Random House Children's Books supports the First Amendment and celebrates the right to read.

Penguin Random House LLC supports copyright. Copyright fuels creativity, encourages diverse voices, promotes free speech, and promotes a vibrant culture. Thank you for buying an authorized edition of this book and for complying with copyright laws by not reproducing, scanning, or distributing any part in any form without permission. You are supporting writers and allowing Penguin Random House to publish books for every reader.

STEP INTO READING®

3 STEP · READING ON YOUR OWN

A HISTORY READER

CHRISTOPHER COLUMBUS

EXPLORER AND COLONIST

by Stephen Krensky

illustrated by Norman Green

Random House 🏠 New York

It is August 3, 1492.
In the Spanish harbor
of Palos,
three ships—
the *Niña*, the *Pinta*,
and the *Santa Maria*—
are starting out to sea.

The sailors on board
are busy with their jobs.
But they do not look happy.
They are nervous.
The ocean is a great mystery.
They have many questions.
How big is it?
How long will they take
to cross it?
What if they get lost?
Will they ever get back to Spain?

Christopher Columbus
does not share their fears.
He is the Italian navigator
of the *Santa Maria*.
He is also the leader
of the voyage.
Columbus has been a mapmaker, too.
Now he plans to be an explorer.

The rulers of Spain—

Queen Isabella and King Ferdinand—

believe in Columbus.

So they are backing the voyage.

Columbus promises to find
a new trade route from Spain
to India, China, and Asian islands.
If he can actually do that,
Spain will become rich.

Until now, European explorers
have always sailed east to Asia.
Columbus knows the world is round.
So he will sail to the west.
No one he knows of has ever
gone that way to the Far East.

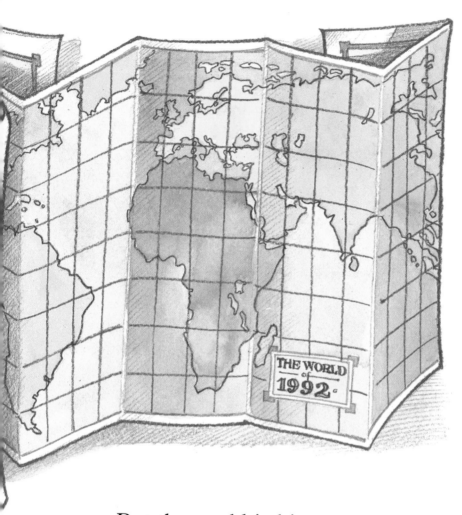

THE WORLD
of
1992

But the world is bigger

than Columbus thinks.

Two huge continents

lie in his path.

People in Europe

don't know they are there.

Soon the sailors cannot see land.

Now they are *really* afraid.

What if the wind stops blowing?

If it does, the ships will stop, too.

What if there is a storm?

The ships are small

and made mostly of wood.

If they are damaged,

no other ship will come

to rescue them.

Luckily, the weather is good.

The wind blows steadily.

The sea is calm.

The ships are loaded

with food and water.

There are extra sails
and spare wood.

They take up a lot of space.

Many sailors must sleep on deck.

There are about ninety men

traveling on the three ships.

Most are sailors,

but there is also a doctor,

a carpenter, a goldsmith, and

an interpreter.

There are even some boys

to help the sailors do their work.

Weeks and weeks go by.

Everyone is growing tired.

Tired of eating salt meat.

Tired of the sun overhead.

Tired of seeing nothing but ocean
around them.

One night, a fiery bolt of light
blazes across the sky.
The sailors watch it fall
into the sea.
Is it a warning sign?
Should they turn back?
Are they going to die?
But Columbus knows
it is just a meteor.
"Sail on!" he tells them.
And on they go.

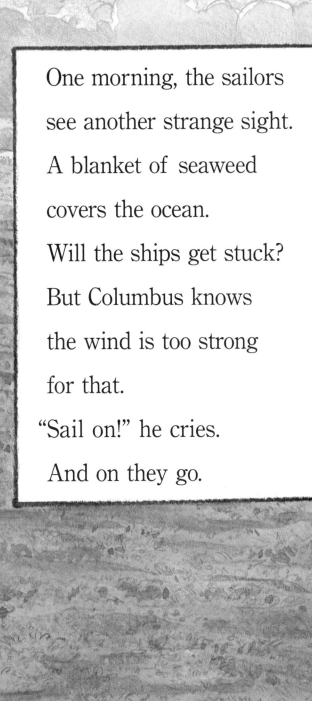

One morning, the sailors
see another strange sight.
A blanket of seaweed
covers the ocean.
Will the ships get stuck?
But Columbus knows
the wind is too strong
for that.
"Sail on!" he cries.
And on they go.

Almost two whole months pass.

The sailors are grumbling.

Where is the land Columbus promised?

Columbus sees some birds

flying overhead.

He points to leafy branches

floating in the water.

Land must be close!

More days go by.

The sailors complain loudly.

No one cares anymore about finding a new route to the Indies.

They just want to stay alive.
Columbus must turn back!
But they are so close, he insists.
He begs them to wait just
three more days.
Finally, they agree.

On the first day and night,
nothing happens.
But on the second night,
the lookout on the *Pinta*
sees the moonlight reflecting
off a sandy beach.
"Land! Land!" he shouts.
The message is sent
from ship to ship.
It is October 12, 1492.

As the sun rises,

everyone can see an island.

This must be the Far East!

Small boats are used to go ashore.

The sailors are so happy

to reach land,

they kiss the sand at their feet.

There are people on the island.
Columbus calls them *Indios*
because he thinks
he has reached the Indies.
He names the island San Salvador.

But the island already
belongs to the Taíno people
who live there.
They call it Guanahani.
Columbus doesn't care.
He says the island
now belongs to Spain.

Columbus trades beads and bells
for cloth and birds.
The Taínos are happy to barter.
But they do not realize
Columbus has now put himself
and Spain in charge of their lives.

The Taínos are wearing gold jewelry.

Columbus uses his hands to ask

where the gold comes from.

But it is hard to communicate.

So Columbus sails farther west

looking for gold.

He visits other islands.

He meets more Taínos.

They live in houses

with thatched roofs of long grasses.

They sleep in rope beds called hammocks.

They travel in long boats called canoes.

Columbus sees many new things.

But he does not see any gold.

And that's what he wants most.

Early one morning,

when a boy holds the tiller,

the *Santa Maria* runs aground.

The ship is wrecked!

Columbus moves to the *Niña*.

But there's not enough room

for everyone.

Many sailors must stay behind.

Soon the *Niña* and the *Pinta*
are ready to sail back to Spain.
The ships are already loaded
with many new kinds of food—
corn, potatoes, peanuts,
papayas, and avocados.
Columbus has also forced
six Taínos to come with them.
He thinks they are his property
and he can do whatever he wants.

On the way home,

the weather changes.

Day after day,

fierce winds batter the ships.

Huge waves crash over the decks.

Even Columbus is afraid

his ship may sink.

On March 15, 1493,
Columbus finally reaches Spain.
The entire voyage has lasted
thirty-two weeks!

Columbus rides from the port

to visit the king and queen.

All along the way,

people gather to cheer him

and to see what

he has brought back.

Columbus is praised far and wide.

The Spanish believe he has found

a new route to the Indies.

Columbus thinks so, too.

He never learns
that these "Indies"
are in a part of the world
that no one in Europe knew about.
It will soon be called America!

Author's Note

The story of Christopher Columbus is really two stories woven together. The first concerns a brave explorer and great navigator who crossed a dangerous ocean and discovered lands he never knew existed. The other story concerns Columbus as a cruel colonizer from Spain, one of many European countries whose rulers believed they could take over such lands and rule their people. Columbus was not the first colonizer of distant lands. Nor was he the last, as colonization continued for hundreds of years.

Both stories, the good and the bad, should be told and remembered. It is also important that we now celebrate Indigenous Peoples' Day on the same date as Columbus Day. It is time to honor the "Indians," the Native Americans who lived here for thousands of years before Columbus ever dreamed of crossing the ocean.